DEDICATION

This book is dedicated to the wild raccoons, opossums, deer, rabbits and birdlife with whom I share my home in Charlotte, North Carolina, USA.

They were here before me. And rather than force them to make way for me and move away, I have chosen to share this space with them.

It has been a learning curve for all of us. And I believe that we are all the richer for this sharing.

Horace made the first overture. I made the first mistake in not understanding his natural instinct to protect what is his. Together we have something special. He remains a wild thing, but he knows my voice, comes when called and gives me as much trust as he can.

To my first grandson, Liam, in the hope that he will come to understand, appreciate, treasure, and protect the beauty of the wildlife with whom he will share this planet.

To my South African artist, Camilla Ridsdale, who so masterfully created the wonderful pen and watercolor illustrations in this book, thank you. Without your talent, this story could never have been told.

Bruce Wm Stewart
Charlotte, North Carolina, USA

My name is Horace and I'm a raccoon. My name was not Horace when I was born. I was just another raccoon. But then I met the man-creatures. And after that, my life changed. Let me tell you my story.

My family live in a small creek that runs along the border of the man-creature's home. We wanted to live by the creek because there's food and water close-by. Water is important for us because we use water to better sense what it is we are eating. While man-creatures use sight and smell to identify food, we use touch and feel, and water is important for this. We also need water to wash our front paws – we simply cannot stand having dirty paws. And of course, there's so much playtime in water.

Shortly after I was born, my dad and his brother took me on a great adventure – a special dinner-date. We left the creek, crossed a large lawn, and climbed up some stairs onto the deck of this really big house.

My dad told me to hide between some pot-plants while he and my uncle checked out the area to see if it was safe for me to come into the open. He stood up and looked through a glass door and the next minute this huge man-creature opened the door and came outside. At first, I was scared of this man-creature. But my dad seemed fine when the man-creature started making noises. He called my dad, Bandit, and my uncle, Zorro, and put down bowls of food and water for them. I suppose the name Bandit and Zorro came from them looking like they are wearing black masks over their eyes. My dad and uncle kept their distance from the man-creature until he had stepped away from the bowls of food and water. The man-creature sat down a short way away from the food and made soothing sounds which my dad seemed to like and trust.

My dad called me and told me it was safe to come out of hiding and to eat food, drink water, and meet this man-creature and soon thereafter, the woman-creature, who also lived here. The food was delicious, and I hoped we would come here again.

Every night my dad and I would go to these man-creatures for food and water, and they seemed to know exactly when we would arrive. In addition to my dad getting the name Bandit, I heard another name – Horace. And this became my name.

And now a strange thing happened. Even though my dad told me that I was a wild animal, that we should avoid humans and that humans were often afraid of us, I felt that this man-creature was different. That he wanted to be with us. But my dad kept telling me to keep my distance from all humans.

One evening my dad was late coming home and I was hungry. I could see and hear that the man-creature and the woman-creature were sitting out on the deck and that the smell of food was really great. So, on my own, I headed across the lawn, up the stairs and onto the deck. But there was no food and water waiting for me. Indeed, the man-creature and woman-creature were so busy talking and eating their own food, that they did not even see me. What was I to do? I was hungry, but there was no food for me. I could smell food on the table where the man-creatures were sitting, but the table was too high for me. So, I did what seemed like a good idea – I grabbed the man-creature's leg – I'm not sure why. Perhaps to use him as a ladder onto the table or perhaps just to give him a hint that "hey pal, have you forgotten your guests?"

The man-creature looked down at me and said "Hello Horace. Welcome to our home. Please join us for dinner." And leaning down he placed bowls of food and water in front of me.

"Wow, this is easy," I thought, as I started to eat the food. "I'll be back tomorrow. Same place, same time."

And then something very strange happened. The man-creature put out his hand and stroked my fur. At first it was a strange feeling. No-one had ever done this to me before.

But soon I got used to this and it felt good. Obviously, the man-creature enjoyed this as well, as every night thereafter we would do the same thing – I'd walk into his house, stand up on my back-legs, hold onto the food bowl, walk out together and he'd stroke my fur while I had supper. Often there would be other man-creatures in the house, but I only trusted the man-creature who made soothing noises to me, fed me and stroked my fur.

Over the next days and weeks, I went to the man-creature every evening, same place, same time. Sometimes he was waiting for me. Sometimes I had to wait for him. But I was hungry and impatient for food, so when I had to wait for him to prepare my food, I figured I might as well go and see where the food came from. So, I just walked into the man-creature's home, stood up on my hind-legs and said "Hey, hurry up! I'm here!"

The man-creature walked towards me with my food. I reached up and grabbed the edge of the bowl and held on. Together, the man-creature and I walked out of his house and onto the deck where we put down the bowl. And the man-creature sat down next to me while I had supper.

This became a nightly routine, and I went to the man-creature's house so often that I left a visible pathway across the lawn between my den and the man-creature's house.

Then one day, I saw the beginnings of another pathway across the lawn. The creek-gang lived further down the creek, and I guess they had learned that the cuisine at my man-creature's house was better than anywhere else.

The first time the creek-gang arrived while I was having supper, I had to hiss at them and chase them away. But they came back later, and because I had left no food for them, they dug up all the flowerpots on the deck, making a terrible mess and making the man-creature very angry.

But one of the creek-gang seemed very nice. She didn't just barge up to my food-bowl and have me hiss and bully her into going way. She just turned her back on me, and slowly reversed up to me, rubbing her back against me, until I got used to her. Then she'd slowly turn around, nuzzling up against me until I felt comfortable that she wanted to share and not take.

And after this, she'd often come to the house after hearing the man-creature call out to me. Sometimes he'd even put down an extra bowl of food for my friend who was now called Lady Grey, after her soft gray fur.

Raccoons are both playful and full of mischief. We play with anything we can find. The man-creatures put a large marble in my water-bowl. And after eating my supper, I'd have a long drink of water and then wash my paws in the water-bowl. I had so much fun playing with the marble, pushing it round and round the bowl.

Now raccoons are not always the tidiest of eaters. We are very good with our front-paws and can sort through food, looking for the best bits. But we also tend to spread around the unwanted bits of food.

And here a friendly Opossum helps out. Penny the Opossum - that's the name that the man-creatures gave her - comes up onto the deck as soon as we leave, and vacuums up all the food that we have left behind.

Penny has a lovely long pointed nose, a long tail and lovely soft gray fur. She has beautiful pink fingers on her front paws and should really be called "trash-can", since she eats pretty much everything and never gets sick. So, all we leave behind is our foot-prints – not a shred of food anywhere and the food-bowl is so clean it may well have come out of the dishwasher.

Opossums are really great to have around your home. They are omnivores and eat just about anything. They are immune to rabies and snake venom. They are also believed to be big eaters of ticks, cutting down on infectious diseases like Lyme disease. And where there are lots of deer, there will be lots of ticks.

And then an accident. I say it was my fault because I should have known better. The man-creature says it was his fault because he should have known better. But it happened – I bit the man-creature and made him very sore. This is what happened.

As usual I went to the house for supper. The man-creature was still making my supper so I went into the kitchen to wait for him, standing up to hold onto the bowl so we could walk out together. He put the bowl down and then did something different. He reached across the bowl to stroke me. He never normally did this. He would always come to my side and stroke me, never reaching across the bowl.

So, I hissed at him to warn him not to come near my food.

He reached across the bowl again and I hissed at him again.

Then he reached across the bowl again and I lunged at him, forgetting that while raccoons have lovely thick fur to protect us, he did not, and my teeth went into his hand. He shouted in pain and with the noise I got scared and ran away.

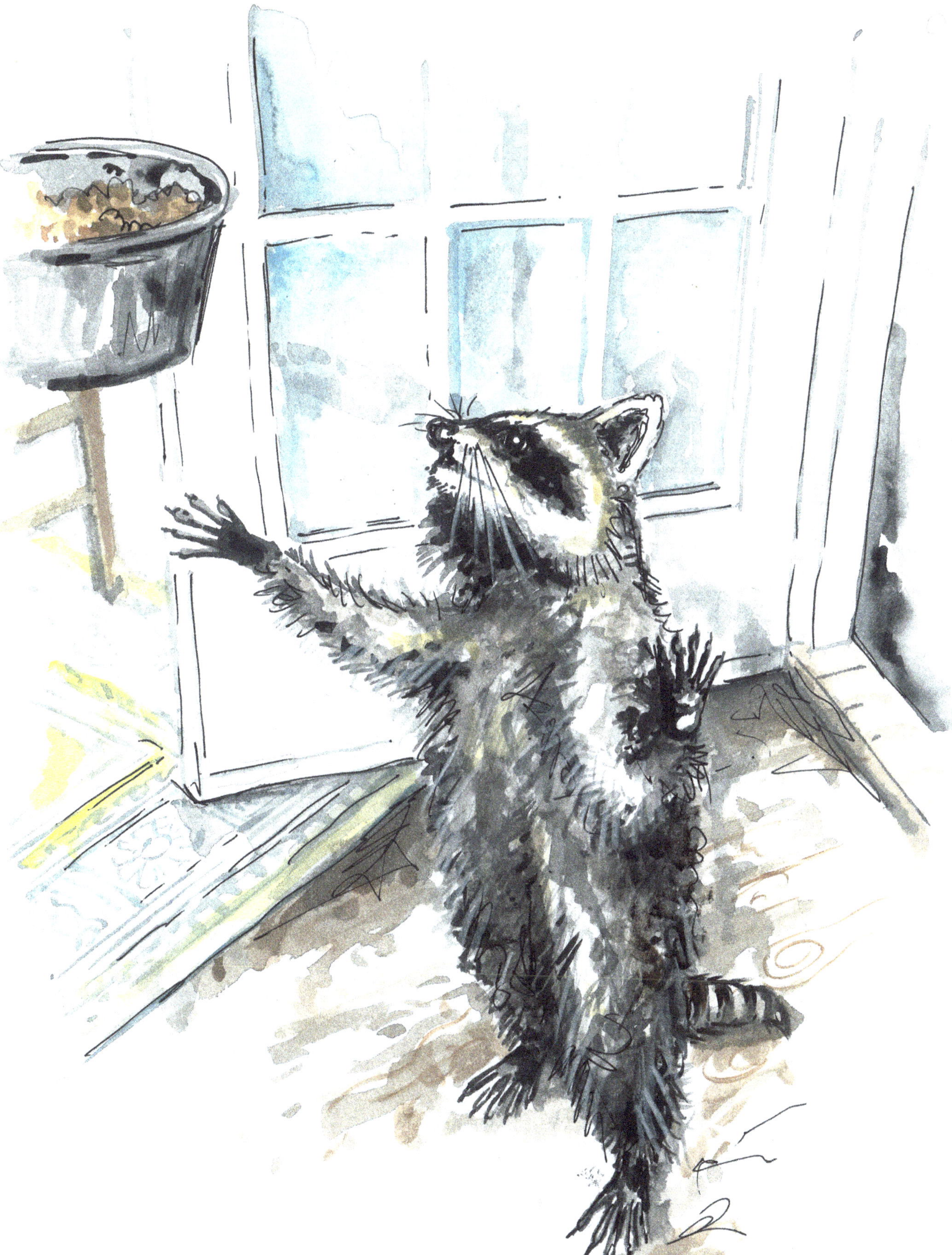

The man-creature went to the hospital to have his hand fixed. The people at the hospital said that Animal Control would come and kill me so they could test whether I had rabies, a disease that's really dangerous to people and animals. They said that since I had bitten the man-creature, I must have rabies. But the man-creature defended me and said it was his fault for reaching across my food-bowl. He showed them photographs of our friendship. Of me in his kitchen and of us holding the bowl together. And of him stroking me. They believed him but said he should have the rabies injections to be on the safe side. All this took a long time at the hospital, and it was many hours before the man-creature came home.

In the meantime, I knew I had done something bad, and I was sorry. I kept going up onto the deck to look for my friend, but he was not there. Eventually I decided to leave him a message and since I could not write or talk, I took the marble out of the water-bowl and left it on the doormat right outside the door, where he would be sure to see it. I hoped the man-creature would understand that it was an accident and that I never intended to hurt him.

For some nights after this, I never went near the man-creature. I think I was afraid that we were not friends anymore. But then I heard him calling. He did not sound angry. So, I went back up onto the deck to see my friend.

But we had both learned a valuable lesson. I am a wild animal. And the way I can interact with other raccoons is different from how I can interact with man-creatures. They can easily get hurt. So, I no longer go into his kitchen. I don't try to hold the food-bowl and he does not try to stroke me. We are close, but we don't get too close. We have reached that understanding. It works for both of us.

And yet, there is still a bond. I come when called and he still feeds me and sits with me and talks to me while I am eating. And sometimes, when he is away and does not bring me food, I take the marble out of the water-bowl and leave it on the mat just outside the kitchen door. It's a message – "Hey man-creature, I was here. Where were you?" And the next evening, he'll be there with an even more special supper for me. A message to me – "Sorry my friend. I was busy. Please forgive me."

There's a lesson here. Raccoons are wild animals. We were here before the man-creatures. We don't have to live together. We just need to understand one another. So, we can enjoy the same space in harmony.

I am now an adult raccoon and I have my own family – four little raccoons that the man-creature calls "floofs" because they are really just little balls of fur. Sometimes I take them up onto the man-creature's deck for some food. But these kits of mine – little man-creatures are called kids, while little raccoons are called kits – are rather mischievous. Instead of eating from the food-bowl, one kit will simply climb into the bowl and then hiss at the others when they try to get to the food. I tried to keep some sort of law and order, but while I was sorting out the naughty kits, another would grab the whole bowl of food and run away. But eventually, everyone had a chance to get some food because the man-creature brought some extra food-bowls for all of us.

Then the kits decided it was play-time. Next to the man-creature's deck is a large fig-tree. Soon the figs will be lovely and ripe and sweet, and we'll climb into the tree to eat the figs. But right now, the figs are hard and green, not good for eating but lovely to play with. And because the figs are not completely round, they will only roll around in circles. The kits have so much fun chasing the rolling figs.

The man-creature also has a birdbath on the deck and to make it look pretty he has put some colored stones and pretty marbles in the birdbath. And of course, the raccoon kits love getting into the birdbath to drink water, wash hands and remove the marbles for some more playtime. But marbles don't roll around in circles – they keep on rolling until they fall off the deck. Well, plenty more where they came from. The kits just go back to the birdbath to get another marble. And the poor man-creature spends so much time collecting the marbles from under the deck to put back into the birdbath.

The other day the man-creature had to go away for a few days, but he was kind enough to arrange for someone else to come and feed me. But this new man-creature was different from my friend. She was the man-creature's kit. And she was grown up and soon to have her own little kit, who she will call Liam.

I wonder whether Liam will also be my friend, like his grandfather.

What do you think?

Let me tell you about the illustrations in this book.

Over the years, the man-creature took many photographs of my raccoon family and the world we live in. Then, when he decided to write this book, he sent the photographs to Camilla in a far-away country, South Africa, where the man-creature once lived with his mate and their kids.

Camilla was fascinated by the photographs because there are no raccoons in Africa, and she had never seen a raccoon. So, Camilla offered to use the photographs to draw the pen and watercolor illustrations for this book.

But we need your help too. In the next few pages, Camilla has drawn the illustrations in pen only. No color. That's your job. To color in the pages, just like Camilla did. You decide what colors to use.

Follow Horace on his Instagram page at
@HoraceTheFriendlyRaccoon
and on his FaceBook page.

For information about ordering this book, contact the author, Dr Bruce Stewart at
www.HoraceTheRaccoon.com

www.ingramcontent.com/pod-product-compliance
Lightning Source LLC
Chambersburg PA
CBHW081410270326
41931CB00016B/3443